# BIG CATS!

## Explore the Fascinating Worlds of . . .

### COUGARS
by Patricia Corrigan

### LEOPARDS
by Kathy Feeney

### LIONS
by Cherie Winner

### TIGERS
by Gwenyth Swain

*Illustrations by John F. McGee*

NorthWord Press
Chanhassen, Minnesota

© NorthWord Press, 2002

Photography © 2002: Claudia Adams/Dembinsky Photo Associates: p. 171; Robert E. Barber/Visuals Unlimited: p. 106; Erwin & Peggy Bauer: pp. 7, 24, 28, 42-43, 58-59, 62-63, 138-139, 180; Craig Brandt: pp. 50, 92; Robin Brandt: p. 136; Alan & Sandy Carey: pp. 57, 155, 160-161, 167, 168-169, 172-173, 174, 182-183; W. Perry Conway: pp. 30-31, 36, 47; Gerald & Buff Corsi/Visuals Unlimited: pp. 126-127; Gerry Ellis/Minden Pictures: p. 131; Michael H. Francis: pp. 8, 10-11, 20-21, 32-33, 38-39, 96, 121; D. Robert & Lorri Franz: p. 146; Mitsuaki Iwago /Minden Pictures: pp. 99, 110, 112, 124; Gavriel Jecan/Art Wolfe, Inc.: pp. 52, 54-55, 80, 114; Adam Jones/Danita Delimont, Agent: pp. 66-67, 156; Brian Kenney: cover, pp. 18, 26-27, 144, 148-149, 150; Rich Kirchner: pp. 105, 109, 116-117, 135; Gary Kramer: pp. 82-83; Frans Lanting/Minden Pictures: pp. 102-103; Tom & Pat Leeson: pp. 14, 34, 37, 44, 90-91, 98, 132-133, 142, 151, 157, 164; Wayne Lynch: pp. 4, 13, 40; Stephen G. Maka: pp. 101, 128; Craig Packer: pp. 122-123; Fritz Polking/Dembinsky Photo Assoc.: pp. 53, 64, 74-75, 78-79, 84; Anup Shah: pp. 61, 65, 70, 73, 86-87, 89, 100, 118-119, 120, 145, 158, 162, 177, 178-179, 184; Anup Shah/Dembinsky Photo Assoc.: pp. 68, 69, 76; Tom J. Ulrich: pp. 16-17; Tom Vezo: pp. 6, 22-23; Terry Whittaker/Dembinsky Photo Associates: p. 181; Art Wolfe: pp. 56, 85, 152-153.

Illustrations by John F. McGee

NorthWord Press
18705 Lake Drive East
Chanhassen, MN 55317
1-800-328-3895
www.northwordpress.com

**Library of Congress Cataloging-in-Publication Data**
Big cats! : explore the fascinating worlds of-- / Patricia Corrigan ... [et al] ; illustrations by John F. McGee.
        p. cm.
  Contents: Cougars / by Patricia Corrigan -- Loepards / by Kathy Feeney -- Lions / by Cherie Winner -- Tigers / by Gwenyth Swain.
  ISBN 1-55971-798-X (hc.)
    1. Puma--Juvenile literature. 2. Leopard--Juvenile literature. 3. Lions--Juvenile literature. 4. Tigers--Juvenile literature. [Puma. 2. Leopard. 3. Lions. 4. Tigers.] I. Corrigan, Patricia II. McGee, John F., ill.
QL737.C23 B56 2002
599.75'5--dc21                                                        2001058664

Printed in Singapore          10  9  8  7  6  5  4  3  2  1

# BIG CATS!

## TABLE OF CONTENTS

*Explore the Fascinating World of...*

# Cougars

**Patricia Corrigan**
**Illustrations by John F. McGee**

COUGARS are seldom seen and rarely heard. In fact, they often live their entire lives unobserved by humans!

But we do know that these members of the cat family live in eleven western U.S. states. They are found from the southernmost tip of Alaska down to where the California border meets Mexico and east all the way to the edge of Texas. Their cousins, Florida panthers, live in Florida. In Canada, cougars are found in British Columbia and parts of Alberta. Cougars also live throughout Mexico, Central America, and South America.

In different areas of the world, cougars have different names. They may be called mountain lions, wildcats, pumas, painters, fire cats, swamp lions, or catamounts. In Mexico, Spanish for cougar is *el león,* which means "the lion." And sometimes they are known by nicknames like "ghost of the wilderness" and "ghost walker."

Cougar eyesight may be five times better than human eyesight.

Males and females look alike, but it is the female that cares for the young.

Like all cats, cougars rest and sleep a lot, maybe as much as 15 to 18 hours each day.

Scientists who study animals are called zoologists (zoe-OL-uh-jists). They think that all cats and dogs may have come from a single tree-dwelling creature that lived 50 million years ago. Some early relatives of the cougar, such as the saber-toothed tiger, have become extinct, or have died out. They did not survive because their environment, or habitat, changed or disappeared.

Fortunately, cougars are able to live in many different habitats. Over time, they have adapted, or evolved, for living in places such as snow-capped mountains, jungles thick with vegetation, cool pine forests, grassy plains, and murky swamps. For instance, cougars that live in northern mountains tend to be larger and have a thicker coat of fur than cougars that live elsewhere. They learned to climb trees. And they also can swim if necessary, but usually prefer to stay dry—like their relative, the house cat!

## Cougars
# FUNFACT:

**Native Americans have always treated the cougar with honor and respect. In times past, cougar skins were used to make arrow quivers and blankets. Claws were used to make necklaces, and sometimes tails were used to decorate clothing.**

Cougars don't hunt from trees, but a high branch makes a good lookout spot.

The average cougar measures from 3.3 to 5.3 feet (1 to 1.6 meters) long and stands about 2 feet (0.6 meter) high at the shoulder. Adult male cougars weigh up to 225 pounds (101 kilograms), and adult females usually are slightly smaller. A cougar's tail may measure up to 32 inches (81 centimeters), almost two-thirds the length of the animal's body.

The cougar is one species (SPEE-sees), or kind, of wild cat. Cougars are medium-sized, along with bobcats and lynxes. Tigers, lions, and leopards all are larger and heavier.

Cougars are muscular and sleek, with little fat on their bodies. Fat usually serves as excellent insulation and keeps an animal's body warm. But because cougars have little of this kind of insulation, they have another natural defense against the cold: their fur coats keep them warm.

No matter the season, cougars are always alert to new things around them.

The layer of hair closest to the skin, called the underfur, is woolly and short. The top layer is made up of longer hairs, called guard hairs. These hairs are hollow and trap the air to keep cold temperatures from reaching the animal's skin.

Unlike humans, cougars have no sweat glands, so the cougars that live in warm climates cool themselves the same way dogs do, by panting to release heat from their bodies.

Cougars' coats are usually tawny, or orange-brown. They also may be gray, sandy brown, reddish-brown, and tan. All adult cougars have black markings on the sides of the muzzle, or snout, where the whiskers are. Some people say this area looks as if the cougar has a "mustache."

Cougars are just as active in winter as summer. The cold weather doesn't prevent them from moving very slowly and quietly.

If cougars were less secretive, scientists might be able to tell individual animals apart by the dark patterns on the muzzles, but few of the animals are ever seen.

The chin is white, as is the area right under the pinkish-brown nose. The tips of their tails also are black. The underside of most cougars is light, sometimes nearly white. At first glance, adult cougars resemble female lions.

Their coloring helps them blend in with their surroundings. It is good camouflage (KAM-uh-flaj) and helps them hide from their prey (PRAY), or the animals they hunt for food.

Cougars have good eyesight. In fact, vision is their best-developed sense. Researchers believe that they can see moving prey from long distances. The cougar's yellow eyes have large, round pupils that take in all available light. That helps the animal see at night almost as well as during the day.

A keen sense of hearing is important for cougars. They even can move their small, rounded ears to take in sounds coming from different directions. Cougars also have a strong sense of smell, which can really be useful when following prey. Still, their sense of smell is not as well developed as their senses of sight or hearing.

## Cougars
# FUNFACT:

A cougar is a "perfect walker." This means that when it's moving along slowly, each hind paw steps in the exact same spot where the front paw had been. When a cougar runs, it's not nearly as careful!

A hungry female with young to feed will even risk getting wet to catch a big fish for dinner.

The Florida panther is smaller than the cougars in the West and has longer legs, smaller feet, and a shorter, darker coat.

Like all of its cat relatives, cougars have whiskers. These sensitive hairs are also called vibrissae (vie-BRIS-ee). They grow on either side of the animal's nose and mouth, above the eyes, and sometimes on the chin.

These whiskers vary in length, but most of the whiskers found on the muzzle are long enough to stretch past the side of the face and back to the edge of the ear. The cougar uses whiskers to gather information through touch. With its whiskers, a cougar can determine the height of the grass, the width of the space under a rock, and whether a bush would be easy or difficult to push through.

Cougars make a variety of sounds, or vocalizations (vo-kul-ize-A-shuns). Their meow, which is a sign of contentment, is much louder than that of a pet cat. They also purr when they are contented. Cougars hiss first and then growl when they feel threatened. Unlike lions, cougars cannot roar. Sometimes the female cougar makes a whining or whistling call to alert males that she is ready to mate, and the male replies with a sound that is close to a screech.

## Cougars
# FUNFACT:

When watching or stalking prey, a cougar may make no sound at all. And it can remain motionless for long periods of time, even up to 30 minutes.

When a cougar sees an enemy nearby, it may try to look ferocious
and scare it away by showing its teeth and growling.

When running very fast, the cougar's whole body stretches out to cover a lot of ground.

The cougar's head is small compared to the rest of its body, but its jaws are powerful.

Like all cats, cougars groom themselves. Grooming helps keep their coats clean. They use their rough tongues to remove any loose hair and to untangle any matted hair. Female cougars groom their babies constantly, and young siblings have been seen grooming one another. Scientists are still unsure whether mating pairs groom one another.

Cougars have very strong jaws. And they have three kinds of teeth, 24 in all. The carnassial (kar-NASS-ee-ul) teeth are located on both the top and bottom jaws. They are long and sharp, used for slicing or shearing. The canine (KAY-nine) teeth are thick and sharp, used for puncturing. The incisors (in-SIZE-ors) are small and straight, used for cutting and some chewing. But cougars don't chew their food very well. They mostly gulp down large chunks.

## Cougars
# FUNFACT:

Sometimes cougars use their long tails to help them balance as they run. When they walk, the tip of the tail may drag on the ground and leave a trail, especially in snow.

Most adult cougars are solitary, which means they live alone. They protect their territory from intruders, including other cougars. Each cougar needs a lot of space, an average of as much as 200 square miles (518 square kilometers) for adult males and less than half that for adult females. They may walk as far as 30 miles (48 kilometers) in a day, searching for food or patrolling their territory.

While on patrol, cougars mark the boundaries of their territory by leaving their scent (SENT), or odor. Cougars may urinate on trees and bushes. Or they may scratch together a small mound of leaves and twigs, called a scrape, and then urinate on top of the mound. Sometimes cougars deposit piles of droppings, or scat, on top of the scrape. Cougar droppings may contain bone and fur. It depends on what the animal has eaten recently. The scrapes are left where they easily will be found by any cougars traveling through the area. Cougars also may reach high up a tree trunk and put claw marks into the bark.

Cougar habitat can be rugged and dangerous to travel.
The cougar's strong legs help it patrol for hours each day.

Large, older cougars usually make longer and deeper scratches than younger or smaller cougars.

Male cougars mark their territory for two reasons. First, they want to warn other males that this land is already taken, and newcomers are not welcome. Zoologists say that other cougars pay attention to these warnings and that rival cougars rarely come face to face. If they do, there may be a fight.

Second, males mark their territory to let females in the area know where to find them for mating. Because female cougars don't require as much space as males, they often choose an area that overlaps a male's territory. Female cougars are ready to mate by the age of two, and in most areas, cougars mate year-round.

After mating, the male and female each return to their separate territories. The female then searches carefully for a protected place, called a den site, where she will later give birth. Sometimes she finds a cave or an opening on a hillside covered by tree roots. Or she just uses a pile of brush in a hidden area.

Small caves on rocky ledges make good den sites.
Sometimes there is only room for the young to crawl inside.

The baby cougars, or kittens, are born about ninety days after the female mates with the male. Usually, she gives birth to two or three kittens, but sometimes the group, or litter, is as large as six.

The newborn kittens have soft, fluffy-looking fur that is speckled with brown spots. This coloring helps camouflage them.

The spots disappear when the kittens are about eight months old. Kittens also have curly tails, which straighten out as they get older.

The kittens are born with blue eyes, which stay closed for about the first two weeks. Their eye color soon changes to yellow.

Kittens are totally dependent on their mother for food. They nurse for up to three months. Immediately after birth, and often in the next few weeks, the female licks the kittens to clean their fur. This helps them stay safe from enemies that might find the den site by detecting the scent of the newborn kittens.

Young kittens stay close to their mother for many reasons,
including food, protection, and warmth.

Mothers pick up their kittens by the scruff of the neck to move them one at a time to a new den site.

If a female cougar thinks that her kittens are in danger in a particular spot, she often finds a new hiding place and moves them. A mother cougar will do whatever is necessary to keep the kittens away from dangerous predators (PRED-uh-torz), or enemies, such as wolves.

When the mother leaves to hunt for food, the kittens stay hidden and quiet at the den site. When the kittens are about two months old, their teeth have grown and they nurse less. Their mother begins to bring them food every two or three days. The mother makes no special effort to catch small prey for her small offspring. At first, the young kittens just want to play with the food, no matter what she brings. One of the first lessons the mother teaches her kittens is how to eat this new food.

By example, she shows them how to bite, how to tear meat off the bone, and how to chew. She also teaches the kittens that their rough tongues are good for cleaning the meat off bones. After about six months the kittens are good at eating this food, and they begin to explore away from the den site.

The kittens stay with their mother for about eighteen months. During this time, she teaches them many things about surviving in their habitat. As the kittens mature, the mother cougar takes them hunting. They learn how to find and carefully follow prey. This is called stalking.

They also learn when to pounce, or jump out suddenly, to capture the prey. They are taught how to hide their kill and protect it from other animals. With a lot of practice, they learn to hunt for themselves.

## Cougars
# FUNFACT:

**A cougar's hind legs are slightly longer than its front legs. Its paw print may be as large as 4 inches (10 centimeters) long and wide.**

This young cougar still has some of its baby spots.
It is practicing stalking its prey.

Then, the young cougars go out on their own to find a territory and a mate. If they find good habitat with plenty of prey animals and water in the area, cougars may live about eight to ten years.

Cougars are carnivores (KAR-nuh-vorz), which means they eat only meat. They are expert hunters with strong legs for climbing and jumping and sharp claws for capturing prey.

On each foot, or paw, cougars have four toes. Each toe has a sharp claw about 1 inch (2.5 centimeters) long. Farther up the back of each front leg, cougars have another sharp claw called a dewclaw. This claw is curved and can be used like a hook to help bring down the prey animal. It also is used to help hold the carcass, or dead body, while the cougar eats.

Cougars may enter the water to catch prey, but they prefer to stay on dry land.

Most of the time the paw claws are tucked inside the toes. This kind of claw is called retractile (ree-TRAK-tul). Cougars walk on the soft pads on the bottom of their paws. They have four toe pads and one heel pad. Technically, they walk on their tiptoes, making little noise as they go.

When a cougar grabs onto prey the claws stick out. Cougars also extend their claws to get good traction when they run. They keep their claws sharp by scratching on trees.

## Cougars
# FUNFACT:

The Florida panther is endangered and rare. There may be as few as 30 adults living in the southern, swampy regions of Florida.

Cougars have good balance and can easily leap over fallen trees
and onto rocks without slowing down.

Tall grass that is nearly the same color as the cougar's coat
makes good camouflage for stalking prey.

Cougars can be active during the day and night. This means they may hunt for food at any time. They may hunt elk and moose, but their favorite prey is whitetail deer.

Like all cats, cougars stalk their prey. Once a deer has been sighted, for example, the cougar crouches down low in the grass or behind a big rock. The cougar silently watches, waiting for the right moment to pounce. The twitching of an ear or the tail is often the only sign that the cougar is there, and those signs are hard to see!

Once the deer is close, the cougar leaps from its hiding place and attacks. Like lions, cougars can run very fast for short distances, perhaps up to 40 miles per hour (64 kilometers per hour). Cougars also can leap 20 feet (6 meters) in a single bound, and jump as high up as 16 feet (5 meters).

A cougar usually attacks from the side or the rear, making the most of the element of surprise. It may jump on a deer's back, hanging on with its sharp claws. Then, with its powerful jaw, the cougar bites the deer in the back of the neck. That bite penetrates the spinal cord, and the deer falls immediately. When a cougar bites through the throat of the deer, the animal suffocates, or stops breathing, and dies.

Next, the cougar drags the carcass to a safe place for feeding. The teeth a cougar chews with are on the sides of its mouth, so it turns its head sideways when eating, just like a house cat. An adult cougar can eat 5 to 15 pounds (2 to 7 kilograms) of meat at one sitting. A whole deer provides meals for several days for a single cougar. A lone male may hunt just once about every fifteen days, but a mother feeding and raising kittens requires more frequent meals.

Cougars don't catch their prey every time. Sometimes the animal is faster and gets away.

Chasing a porcupine up a tree is one way to capture food.
But it's not an easy way to get a meal.

Sometimes the cougar hides a carcass from other animals by covering it with branches and grasses. Or it may dig a hole and bury the carcass as extra protection. Just to be sure no other animal steals its meal, the cougar may sleep nearby, in case it has to defend its food from bears or other large animals.

When deer are not available, cougars hunt small mammals such as squirrels, raccoons, chipmunks, coyotes, foxes, rabbits, marmots, rats, and mice. A very hungry cougar even will eat porcupines, which can be tricky because of the sharp quills. Those quills hurt when they stick in a cougar's soft nose, so the cougar has to be very careful! The Florida panther prefers deer, opossums, and wild pigs.

At one time, cougars lived in almost every state in America. Early settlers in the East did not like sharing the land with cougars, as the cougars killed deer that the people needed for food. To protect their families, settlers killed many cougars. As more people settled in cougar territory, the habitat was destroyed, and many more cougars died. Today, cougars are endangered, which means we must take extra care to protect them.

Conservationists (con-ser-VAY-shun-ists) are people who care about helping wildlife. Fortunately, they are working to increase the number of cougars and panthers. So, even though you may never see one of these secretive cats in their natural habitat, you will know they continue to share our wild world.

## Cougars
# FUNFACT:

Originally, the Latin name for the cougar was *Felis concolor* (FEE-lis CAWN-color), In 1993, scientists changed it to *Puma concolor* (POO-muh CAWN-color).

Cougars use their keen vision and concentration for watching over their home territory.

# My BIG CATS! Adventures

The date of my adventure: _____

The people who came with me: _____

_____

Where I went: _____

What big cats I saw:

_____     _____

_____     _____

_____     _____

_____     _____

The date of my adventure: _____

The people who came with me: _____

_____

Where I went: _____

What big cats I saw:

_____     _____

_____     _____

_____     _____

_____     _____

# My BIG CATS! Adventures

The date of my adventure: _____

The people who came with me: _____

_____

Where I went: _____

What big cats I saw:

_____          _____

_____          _____

_____          _____

_____          _____

---

The date of my adventure: _____

The people who came with me: _____

_____

Where I went: _____

What big cats I saw:

_____          _____

_____          _____

_____          _____

_____          _____

*Explore the Fascinating World of . . .*

# Leopards

**Kathy Feeney**
**Illustrations by John F. McGee**

HAVE YOU EVER HEARD of a wild cat called "Prima Ballerina" or "Prince of Cats"? These are nicknames for the leopard. It is one of the world's six big cats, along with lions, tigers, cheetahs, cougars, and jaguars. They all are related, and they belong to the scientific classification, or group, called Felidae (FEE-lih-dee). This is the Latin word for "cat family."

The name leopard comes from the Latin words *leo*, which means lion,

and *pard*, which means panther. Scientists use the Latin name *Panthera pardus*, or "the leopard panther." Most people usually shorten it to just "leopard."

Leopards have roamed the Earth since the days of the dinosaur. Scientists have identified leopard fossils that are two million years old. Today, leopards live in parts of Africa, the Middle East, India, China, Siberia, and southeast Asia.

Keen eyesight is one of the leopard's senses that helps it find food and stay alert for nearby enemies.

Young leopards soon learn to find a good place to rest or take a quick nap.

Leopards can adapt, or change, to live in many kinds of places, called their habitat. They always choose habitats that provide plenty of food and shelter. Leopards may be found in tropical rain forests, snowy mountains, jungles, and the wide-open grasslands called savannahs.

You may think it would be simple to see leopards in the wild. But their speckled coloring helps to camouflage (KAM-uh-flaj), or hide, them. Leopards blend into their surroundings and can become nearly invisible in the trees, rocks, and long grass where they live.

## Leopards
# FUNFACT:

Antarctica is the only place on Earth that has no members at all of the whole cat family.

To help protect themselves while getting a drink out in the open, away from good camouflage, leopards stay low to the ground.

The snow leopard has an excellent breathing system. The very cold air is warmed through its nostrils before it goes into the lungs.

There are three types, or species (SPEE-sees), of leopards. They are the snow leopard, the clouded leopard, and the "true" leopard. Snow leopards are found in the mountains of central Asia. They have very large paws, or feet, which act like snowshoes to help them walk on top of the deep snow. When the winter becomes too harsh, snow leopards often move to lower land, where there are more trees for protection from the weather. They have long grayish coats, or fur, with scattered black spots and a long bushy tail. They sometimes use their tails to cover their faces for added insulation in cold temperatures.

Adult snow leopards measure up to 7 feet (2 meters) from nose to tail, and weigh up to 155 pounds (70 kilograms). Their light color helps them hide in the snow of their habitat.

Clouded leopards usually hunt from trees in the daylight. They often hunt on the ground beginning around sunset.

Clouded leopards live in the rain forests of southeast Asia. They are gray or yellow with black and brown spots. They also have some stripes on their heads. An adult is smaller than the other leopard species. It is about 6 feet (1.8 meters) long from nose to tail. Clouded leopards weigh between 35 and 55 pounds (16 and 25 kilograms).

They are named after their spot patterns, which look like groups of clouds. The clouded leopard is also known as the "mint leopard," because some people think its spots look like mint leaves. These same markings help clouded leopards disappear into the tree branches, where they spend much of their time. This is the species most likely to hunt from trees, and ambush an animal on the ground below.

The "true" leopard is the one that most people recognize. This species is found in the wild from South Africa to east of Russia. Adult male leopards are usually 7 feet (2 meters) long from their noses to their tails. They can weigh from 150 to 200 pounds (68 to 90 kilograms). A full-grown female averages 5 feet (1.5 meters) in length and weighs from 80 to 150 pounds (36 to 68 kilograms). Females of all the leopard species are usually smaller than the males.

Depending on the species, a leopard's coat may be a different color, from grayish to pale yellow to tan to gold. But all leopards have spots. Each animal has its own unique spot pattern, just as every human has his or her own unique fingerprints. These spot patterns are often used by scientists who study animals, called zoologists (zoe-OL-uh-jists), to identify individual leopards.

Leopards have good balance, even on slippery rocks crossing a stream. Their tails help them keep their balance.

Some people mistake leopards for cheetahs or jaguars. All three of these cats are nicknamed "the sports cars of cats," because they are sleek, swift, and spotted. But once you compare them side-by-side, it's easy to tell them apart by their spots.

The cheetah has solid black spots that look like polka dots all over its body. The spots on leopards and jaguars are grouped in circles. These markings are called rosettes, because they look like rings of blooming roses. To tell the difference between these two animals, just look at the color in the center of the rosette. Jaguars have rosettes with brownish hair in the center and a black spot. The middle of a leopard's rosette is just plain, brownish hair.

The leopard's fur is thick and soft. Its head and legs have solid black spots. Its undercoat, or belly, is pure white. Leopards have a long spotted tail with a white tip.

Jaguar

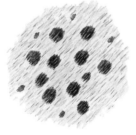

Cheetah

Leopard

If an enemy approaches, such as this hyena, a leopard may quickly jump up into a tree, where its spots still work like camouflage.

A black leopard may have an advantage in hunting because its dark color acts as better camouflage in the low-light conditions of its home in the rain forest.

Some leopards are pure black. They are called panthers. But they are not a separate species. Even though their spots are difficult to see, they do have them. These black leopards can be born into a litter, or group, of babies that also has members with gold, beige, or gray coats. They grow up just like their siblings, or brothers and sisters. The only difference between them is their coat color.

## Leopards
# FUNFACT:

**A leopard is 10 times stronger than a human of the same weight. Its sense of hearing is approximately two times stronger than a human's hearing.**

A mother and her young sometimes find good resting places in the same tree.

The size, weight, and coat color of a leopard also depends on where the animal lives. Light-colored leopards usually live in grassland regions with a few clumps of trees. Leopards found in the desert are sandy colors, such as cream and yellowish brown. Golden-colored leopards live in forest habitats and use the tree shadows to help camouflage themselves. Panthers usually live in jungles where their black coats help them disappear into dark shadows.

Leopards have strong, thick necks and faces with high cheekbones and golden, oval-shaped eyes. Their ears are rounded and their noses are long and wide.

Leopards have broad chests and powerful, short legs for animals of their size. They can run in short sprints up to 37 miles (60 kilometers) per hour.

Leopards also climb trees, where they hide, rest, sleep, and store their food. They often spend time in trees to avoid the insect pests that may be in the grass below. If a leopard feels threatened by a predator, or enemy, it will usually run away or escape to safety up a tree, rather than fight.

These leopard babies already look like their mother,
and will grow quickly and soon be as large she is.

Leopards can move very quickly when they are hunting for food.
And they have good concentration to secretly follow their prey.

Like all members of the cat family, leopards seem to be walking on their tiptoes. This is called digitigrade walking. Leopards actually walk on soft, cushioning pads underneath their toes and on the soles of their paws. They have five toes on their front paws and four toes on their back paws. The pads are surrounded by short, thick fur that helps the leopard keep its balance on slippery rocks and in trees. Both the pads and this extra fur also help the leopard travel silently to surprise the animals they hunt for food, called prey (PRAY).

This leopard is leaving a message for other leopards, "Stay away! This is my home."

Just like one of its other relatives, the house cat, leopards have needle-sharp, curved claws, which they can retract, or pull back, into their paws. The leopard's claws are about 1 inch (2.5 centimeters) long. They are usually retracted to protect them from wearing down or becoming injured. Leopards keep their claws sharp by scratching them on rough surfaces such as tree trunks. Claws are used as weapons for fighting, and as tools for catching and holding prey. They are also used to communicate messages to other leopards by scratching marks on tree trunks.

Leopards are nocturnal (NOK-turn-ul) animals, which means they are more active at night. That is when they travel, hunt, and feed. They are rarely seen in daylight hours. During the day they usually sleep in trees or bushes to keep cool and safely hidden. They may also sun themselves on rocks and sometimes eat the meat from an earlier hunt.

If a leopard senses danger nearby, it may try to scare the enemy away by looking ferocious and showing its teeth.

Leopards have excellent senses of hearing, sight, and smell. They have the best night vision of the six big cats and can locate their prey in almost complete darkness. A leopard's vision may be as much as seven times better than a human's eyesight.

The leopard can see so well in the dark because it has reflective, or mirror-like, layers at the back of its eyes. In bright light, the leopard's pupils become narrow slits. The pupil is the black circle in the center of each eyeball. In dark surroundings the pupils open wide to let in the most light possible. This is when the leopard's eyes appear to glow in the dark.

This leopard is carefully watching and listening to something in the distance. Its whiskers will move depending on whether it feels safe or threatened.

The leopard's long, white whiskers are stiff, sensitive hairs that help it feel its way in the dark. Like other members of the cat family, leopards have whiskers, called vibrissae (vie-BRISS-ee), in three separate places on the head. Some whiskers grow above the eyes. Some are located behind the leopard's cheeks. And very long whiskers grow on each side of the muzzle, at the front.

A leopard's vibrissae can point in different directions, depending on how the animal is feeling and what it is doing.

When leopards are at rest, their whiskers point sideways. When excited or threatened, their whiskers stick upward. When they are hunting and traveling, their whiskers spread out and fall forward in the shape of a fan. This position allows the whiskers to work like radar so the leopard can avoid bumping into things in the dark. The whiskers help tell the leopard the best spot on its prey to make a deadly bite. The whiskers sense when the prey's nerves have stopped twitching and the animal is dead.

The leopard's thin, dark tail may be up to 3 feet (0.9 meter) long. That's longer than your whole arm. Sometimes, the tail is just as long as the whole rest of the leopard's body. The leopard swishes its tail before it leaps or runs. This back and forth movement helps the leopard keep its balance. A female leopard also uses her tail as a flag that her babies, or cubs, can follow when they travel.

The leopard is an excellent swimmer. But it does not spend time in water to cool off. Leopards usually visit a watering hole for a daily drink, even though they can live without water for as long as a month. Leopards do not need to drink often because they get liquids from eating prey.

Leopards are carnivores (KAR-nuh-vorz), or meat-eaters. But they are not picky about their food. The leopard's diet includes many creatures, from tiny insects to large mammals. The menu may include beetles, ostriches, porcupines, rodents, and reptiles. Antelope, deer, jackals, monkeys, and young zebras and cheetahs are also favorite prey animals.

Leopards also eat fish and some fruit. And they are scavengers (SKAV-en-jers), often feeding on carrion (KARE-ee-un), which are animals that are already dead.

## Leopards
# FUNFACT:

**To stay healthy, females should eat approximately 6 pounds (2.7 kilograms) of meat every day. Males require nearly 8 pounds (3.6 kilograms) per day.**

Sometimes a cub's curiosity makes it explore new things.
The turtle inside this shell is probably safe.

Before long, these young leopards from the same litter will separate to hunt and live on their own.

While cubs are still young, their mothers groom them.
They will soon learn to clean themselves.

Leopards have powerful jaw muscles and 32 teeth for crushing bones and tearing flesh. They use their teeth as weapons to grab onto the neck or head of their prey and then snap the animal's spine. Four canine teeth, which are 2 inches (5 centimeters) long, are used for biting and piercing. Curved and pointed like fangs, these teeth work like scissors to cut off pieces of meat, which are swallowed whole without chewing. A leopard can rip off its prey's fur by using its upper and lower front teeth, called incisors.

The leopard's tongue is rough and covered with hook-shaped spikes called papillae (puh-PILL-uh). These sharp bristles can be used by the leopard to scrape flesh from the bones of its prey. The tongue's papillae also come in handy for grooming, or cleaning, the leopard's fur. The mother grooms her babies often to keep them clean. This is very important so the cubs do not attract enemies by their scent, or odor.

Leopards silently stalk, or hunt, their prey. They stay hidden by lying flat on the ground and slowly creeping forward, sneaking up on their prey. When the leopard is about 15 feet (4.5 meters) away, it springs forward and pounces, or jumps, on the animal. Leopards sometimes wait patiently at waterholes for prey animals. They also follow the prey's tracks on the ground. Or the leopard pounces on prey from a hiding place high up in a tree. Leopards usually choose to attack young, sick, or older animals that are easier to catch.

## Leopards
# FUNFACT:

Many legends tell tales of the intelligence and cunning of the leopard. One says that to hide its tracks from predators, the leopard uses its tail to brush away its pawprints in the dirt or sand.

Leopards do not catch every prey animal they stalk and chase.
This gazelle is very fast and may escape.

If the kill is large, such as this warthog, the leopard must use all its strength to drag the prey up a tree to safety.

After each kill the leopard rips open the belly of its prey to remove the stomach and intestines. The leopard covers these organs with dirt, and eats the liver, kidney, and heart of its prey first. Then it eats the meat. Male leopards can go about three days without eating. Females with cubs need to eat nearly every day.

After feasting, a leopard drags the remains of the animal by the neck and pulls it high up into a tree. Leopards have been seen dragging 150-pound (68-kilogram) carcasses up trees that are as tall as two-story buildings.

The leopard hangs its prey over tree branches so the food won't be stolen by other animals looking for a meal. These scavengers include lions, hyenas, and vultures. The leopard can then safely leave, and return whenever it needs a meal. In desert habitats, leopards hide their food among rocks.

Their fierce hunting ability has given leopards a ferocious reputation. But they are really shy and peaceful mammals. Leopards are solitary, which means they prefer to live alone.

Leopards most often try to hide from their enemies, such as baboons, lions, tigers, and hyenas.

Leopards are also quiet animals. They don't make many vocalizations (vo-kul-ize-A-shuns), or sounds. Once in a while they cough, grunt, or can let out a low purr that sounds like a person sawing wood. Females let males know they are ready to mate by making loud growls. Leopard cubs make meowing sounds to call to their mother.

Male and female leopards are both territorial, which means they fiercely protect their territory, or home range. Depending on the food available, males may claim a home range as large as 11 square miles (30 square kilometers). That's about the size of a small town. Females usually live in smaller ranges that overlap with several other females' areas.

Male territories often overlap several female territories without problems. But if two male leopards try to live in one home range, they will probably fight. The loser of the fight must leave the area.

Leopards warn other animals to stay out of their territory by scent marking. Leopards do this by spraying their urine on trees, plants, and rocks. They also claw trees to make "keep out" or "no trespassing" signs.

Leaving scat, or droppings, is another way the animals claim their territory. Also, a male leopard can smell these signs and know if a female is ready to mate.

This leopard has just sprayed a tree trunk.
It will move on to mark other trees in its territory.

Unlike many other animals, leopards do not have one special time to breed. They mate year-round. Males become ready to mate around age three. Females are ready at age two. Female leopards usually give birth every two years.

After mating, a male and female go their separate ways. The male returns to his territory, leaving the female with the responsibility to raise and teach their offspring how to hunt for prey and survive in the wild.

The female leopard soon begins to prepare a den for her young in a cave, a hollow tree, or a thicket of plants. The cubs are born about three months later.

Female leopards usually have one to three cubs in a litter. Newborn leopards weigh about 1.5 pounds (680 grams). The cubs do not leave the den during their first two months. And their mother leaves them only for short periods of time to find food for herself.

This cub is old enough to begin exploring outside the den. Its first journey will be with its mother, and not far from the den.

Cubs need lots of rest to grow strong. They stay close to their mother for warmth, protection, and food.

As they grow, the cubs become playful and curious. Sometimes they try to explore on their own beyond the den. The mother leopard works hard to keep her babies safe from predators. If she senses danger, she carries them by the scruff of their neck, one by one, to a new hiding place. The leopard cub's enemies include adult male leopards, lions, tigers, pythons, baboons, and hyenas. The first year of life is a very dangerous time for the cubs, and they must learn quickly how to stay safe. About half of the leopard cubs that are born each year do not survive to become adults.

Leopard cubs are born with very woolly coats. At birth, their teeth are already starting to push through their gums. They are born with their eyes closed, but at about 14 days old, they open their eyes, which are light blue.

Mother leopards must have patience with young cubs as they play.
Sometimes their jumping games are rough and fast.

The babies drink their mother's milk until they are nearly six weeks old. Then their mother begins feeding them regurgitated, or chewed and spit out, pieces of meat.

By the time they are four months old, the young leopards look like miniature versions of their mother. Their eyes have turned golden and their coats are short, shiny, and spotted. By six months old, the young leopards learn how to hunt. Their mother teaches them where to find prey and how to climb trees. These are difficult things to learn and the cubs must practice many times. Sometimes they try their new skills by stalking and pouncing on each other.

## Leopards
# FUNFACT:

**Even leopards take "catnaps" during the day when they get tired.**

For a few more months, leopard cubs play by hunting mice and insects, but they mostly share their mother's meals. When they are nearly a year old their mother allows them to kill their own prey on a real hunt.

Female leopards hold their tails upright, high in the air, when they are traveling with their cubs. The cubs usually follow behind the mother in a single-file line. The young leopards can keep track of their mother by watching the white tip of her tail as they move around.

Young leopards live with their mothers for nearly two years before leaving to be on their own. Even then, siblings sometimes stay together for several more months before separating to claim their own territories. Sometimes females choose territories near their mother's home range. Young males usually travel farther away from where they were born.

Leopards can live to be 10 to 15 years old in the wild. Many things can affect their lifespan. Leopards can die from starvation and natural disasters, such as floods and forest fires. Some are also killed by other animals including hyenas and lions.

This cub needed some help getting back to the den. It doesn't hurt it to travel this way.

This snow leopard is using its strong leg muscles to run and jump over the snow. Its whole body is stretched out to cover more ground.

Climbing trees is as easy for leopards as walking on the ground.
High up on a narrow limb is a safe place to relax.

Humans are among the leopard's top enemies. Although the leopard is a protected species and it is illegal to kill them for their fur, thousands of the animals are still hunted each year by poachers. In some countries, claws and whiskers are made into potions and medicine.

Leopards need plenty of open space to roam and hunt. But they often lose their natural habitats when humans build homes in the leopard's territory.

Leopards in the southern half of Africa are a threatened species. This means their population is being closely studied. All other leopards in the wild are endangered, which means they are near to becoming extinct, or gone forever.

Through research, people who want to protect wildlife, called conservationists, gather information that will help leopards. Then they provide the information to others so they can learn new things about this secretive mammal. With the help of these caring humans, leopards will survive in the wild for many years to come.

## Leopards
# FUNFACT:

**Scientists say the leopard
is the most widely distributed
of the six big cats.
The worldwide population
is estimated to be about
600,000 in the wild.**

# My BIG CATS! Adventures

The date of my adventure: _____

The people who came with me: _____

_____

Where I went: _____

What big cats I saw:

_____    _____

_____    _____

_____    _____

_____    _____

The date of my adventure: _____

The people who came with me: _____

_____

Where I went: _____

What big cats I saw:

_____    _____

_____    _____

_____    _____

_____    _____

# My BIG CATS! Adventures

The date of my adventure: _____

The people who came with me: _____

_____

Where I went: _____

What big cats I saw:

_____        _____

_____        _____

_____        _____

_____        _____

---

The date of my adventure: _____

The people who came with me: _____

_____

Where I went: _____

What big cats I saw:

_____        _____

_____        _____

_____        _____

_____        _____

*Explore the Fascinating World of . . .*

# Lions

**Cherie Winner**
**Illustrations by John F. McGee**

THE STORY OF LIONS is filled with danger. It is a story of fierce battles over territory and who will mate. It is a story of hunting for food and survival.

The lion is often called the "King of the Jungle." But lions don't live in jungles. They live on grassy plains, where they hunt antelopes, zebras, and other animals. They also live in areas called open forests, where trees mix with the grassland.

Lions once lived in Africa, Europe, the Middle East, and southern Asia. As humans built towns and farms in these areas, many lions were killed. Others died because they could no longer find enough food. Some moved to places where there weren't so many people.

Today lions live in a much smaller area than they once did. About 21,000 lions still roam in eastern and southern Africa. Only about 200 Asian lions still live in the Gir National Park and Lion Sanctuary in western India.

Lions have keen eyesight
to help them hunt.

Females are very protective of their babies,
and watch over them very carefully.

This resting Asian male lion may not look dangerous, but he becomes extremely fierce when he must protect his territory, or home area.

The lion's scientific name is *Panthera leo*. Lions belong to the Felidae (FEE-lih-dee), or cat, family. They are the second-largest members of the cat family, after tigers. In Africa, adult male lions stand about 48 inches (1.2 meters) high at the shoulder and weigh about 420 pounds (189 kilograms). Females are smaller. They grow to 44 inches (1.1 meters) tall and weigh about 275 pounds (124 kilograms). In India, male lions weigh about 400 pounds (180 kilograms) and females weigh about 250 pounds (113 kilograms).

This female is almost completely camouflaged as she watches for enemies as well as food.

Most lions have golden fur that works like camouflage (KAM-uh-flaj) to blend in with the long grasses. Some lions have dark brown fur, and some are much lighter in color, almost white. A lion's belly and chest are also light, often white.

Whatever the color, lion coats have two layers, a soft layer of thick underfur covered by coarse outer guard hairs. These layers protect lions from harsh sun, chilly winds, and soaking rain. Their lips are black, and their eyes are dark yellow. Many lions have a narrow patch of pale hair just under the eyes.

These young lions have found a good place to rest, high off the ground.

All lions have a long tail with a tuft of black hair at the tip, like a paintbrush. The tail is just long enough to touch the ground when the lion stands up. When a lion runs, it holds the tail up or to one side to help it keep its balance.

Lions are the only cats that have a mane, which is a ring of bushy hair on the head, neck, and shoulders. Maybe it is the mane that makes a lion look like a "king." Only males have a mane. It develops as the young male lion becomes an adult.

The mane can be the same color as the lion's back, or it might be silver, orange, or very dark brown. Strong males usually have a long, dark mane. It is important for a female to mate with a strong male, so their offspring will be strong, too. The bushier, darker mane attracts her to the best choice.

Some African lions have such thick manes that it's hard to see their ears. The manes of Asian lions aren't as bushy, so their ears can easily be seen. In both kinds of lions, the front of each ear is about the same color as the lion's back, or a little lighter. On the back of each ear is a broad stripe or patch of black fur.

The ears are round, and they face forward most of the time. Lions don't often turn their ears to hear better, as many other animals do. They do turn their ears to the back or to the side to warn other lions to stay away. When they turn their ears, the black fur on the back of the ears can be seen.

## Lions
# FUNFACT:

**Young lions sometimes climb trees, but adult lions in the wild seldom do.**

Grooming, or cleaning, is important for lions. They regularly clean themselves with their rough tongues. Sometimes they clean each other.

Along both sides of the lion's long snout are several rows of whiskers. These are long, sensitive hairs that help the lion navigate, or find its way, at night. If a lion walks so close to a tree or a boulder that its whiskers touch it, the lion will turn a bit so it doesn't run into the object.

On the face near the whiskers are several rows of small, black spots. They make a pattern that is different for every lion, just as fingerprints are different for every person. Scientists who study animals are called zoologists (zoe-OL-uh-jists). They use these spot patterns to identify individual lions.

The hair on a lion's face is quite short, but the hair of the mane often grows to 20 inches (51 cm) long.

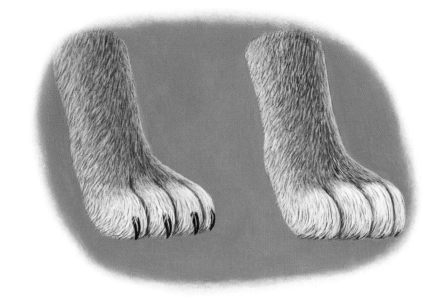

Zoologists also study other parts of the face to learn how old the lion is. If its teeth are yellow and worn down, the lion is probably over 12 years old. The color of the tip of the nose gives clues, too. Young lions' noses are pink and black. As they get older, the black areas get bigger until finally, sometime after they turn five years old, the whole tip of the nose is black.

You can tell by looking at their claws and teeth that lions are carnivores (KAR-nuh-vorz), or meat eaters. They are also predators (PRED-uh-tors), which means they catch and kill the animals they eat, called prey (PRAY).

The long, sharp claws curve downward so the lion can hold on to the prey animal. When a lion is resting, its claws are tucked inside its toes. When it grabs the prey, special muscles make the claws stick out. This kind of claw is called retractile (ree-TRAK-tul). Lions also use their claws to get good traction when they run. They keep their claws sharp by scratching on trees.

A lion has 30 teeth in all. The long, pointed canine (KAY-nine) teeth at the front corners of the mouth are very important. Each lion has two canine teeth in the upper jaw and two in the lower jaw. Lions use their canine teeth to get a good grip on their prey so it can't escape. Their jaws are very strong. Lions usually kill their prey by suffocating it. That means they keep it from breathing. They do this by biting through the throat or by grabbing on to the snout. Either way, the prey cannot breathe and dies quickly.

Farther back in the lion's mouth are four large teeth with jagged edges, called carnassial (kar-NASS-ee-ul) teeth. There are two carnassials on each side of the mouth, one in the upper jaw and one in the lower jaw. When the lion bites down, these teeth work like scissors to cut through the meat. The lion's other teeth are also sharp and help the lion hold on to prey and tear meat.

## Lions
# FUNFACT:

You can tell if an adult lion has been in the area by the signs it leaves on the ground. Each paw print is about the size of a saucer or small plate. A lion's scat, or dropping, is about the size and shape of a banana.

A lion's canine teeth may be 2 to 2½ inches (5 to 6 cm) long.
It can open its jaw 11 inches (28 cm) wide.

When a herd of cape buffalo notices a group of lions hunting in the area, they fiercely protect themselves and their young.

The kind of meat they eat depends on how healthy the lions are and how many lions are hunting. Lions get about one-fourth of their meat by scavenging (SKAV-en-jing), or eating prey that was killed by other animals. Lions will chase hyenas, cheetahs, or other smaller predators away from their kills and steal the food. This seems like an easy way to eat, but the lions never know when they will find such a meal. They usually rely on their hunting skills to catch their own dinner.

Lions that are old or weak usually hunt small prey such as rabbits, birds, or snakes. Healthy lions hunting alone usually go for larger prey such as zebra and antelope. Lions in groups will even hunt big animals like hippopotamuses or cape buffalo.

Lions find their prey mostly by sight and by sound. Lions can see and hear much better than humans can. Their sense of smell is much less important for their hunting than it is for many other wild animals. When hunting during the day or early evening, lions rely mostly on their keen vision to see prey in the distance. When hunting in the dark, their hearing also becomes important. But even then, they depend on their eyesight. Lions can see so much better at night than the animals they are hunting, that they have a big advantage.

Lions also know where prey are most likely to be. Water holes are favorite hunting spots. There aren't many places to find water on the plains, so a good water hole, which is like a large pond, attracts many animals every day. Lions know that if they wait long enough at a water hole, they will have a chance to catch a big dinner.

Because zebras can run for long distances, a lion's best hunting strategy is to surprise the zebra and catch it quickly.

A lion's top speed is about 40 miles (64 kilometers) per hour, but only for short distances. Many prey animals can easily outrun a lion. Fortunately, lions have other skills that are important for hunters. They can change direction or stop in an instant. They are also very patient and very powerful. Sometimes a lion will stalk, or quietly follow, its prey. They usually don't stalk for a long time. Instead of following their prey over long distances, they hide in long grass until the prey comes close. Then they jump out of their hiding place. Lions can leap about 40 feet (12 meters) in one bound. Within a few strides they catch the startled prey.

Sometimes lions cooperate, or work together, to bring down the prey. Several lions may surround the prey, gradually closing in on it. Or one lion may chase the prey toward other lions hiding in the grass or behind large rocks.

## Lions
# FUNFACT:

Lions hunting in pairs or groups catch their prey about 1 time in 3 tries. Lions hunting alone need to try about 6 times to get their dinner.

Even while taking a refreshing drink at a water hole, lions are always watching for possible prey nearby. Lions can swim, but they usually avoid it.

When a lion hunts alone and kills a small prey, it usually keeps it to itself. If a lion kills a large prey, or if two or more lions team up during the hunt, other members of the family group, or pride, come to share the feast. Many lions crowd around the meat, each one trying to get as much of it as possible. Females let the young lions, or cubs, eat at the same time, but male lions sometimes keep other members of the pride away until they are full. Cubs may have to wait for their turn.

When they make a big kill, lions gorge themselves, or eat as much as they can. After the big meal, lions might not hunt and eat again for several days. In the meantime, all members of the pride sleep a lot. In fact, lions sleep or rest for about 19 hours of every day. That is why lions have the reputation for being lazy!

The females of a pride often rest together. They prefer to find a
high place where they can see in all directions.

All the female lions in a pride are related. They are sisters, mothers, daughters, aunts, cousins, or nieces to each other. A female lion, or lioness, lives her whole life in the pride she was born into.

Young males always leave their birth pride when they are about three years old. They go looking for another pride to live with, in order to mate and produce offspring.

Some prides have just one adult male and two adult females and their cubs. Other prides have up to 30 members. Most have around 15 members. Areas with more prey have bigger prides.

Within the pride, different jobs are done by different lions. Females do most of the hunting. Males patrol the pride's territory and defend it against other male lions.

Pages 118-119: These two strong males are traveling together, patrolling their territory.

This lioness can warm herself in the sun while she watches over her territory.

A territory is the area where the pride lives and hunts. In places with lots of prey, it may be only 25 square miles (65 square kilometers). In places with less prey, a lion must search farther for food. The territory might be as large as 250 square miles (648 square kilometers). The lions move around within their territory to follow the prey. They go where the prey animals go.

Lions guard their territory by roaring and by scent (SENT) marking. A roar is a deep, loud sound. It is the loudest sound made by any kind of cat. It is even louder than a jackhammer or a sandblasting machine. A lion's roar can be heard up to 5 miles (8 kilometers) away.

Moving across the savanna in search of food, lions move quietly. They really walk on their toes, making good use of the cushioned pads on their paws.

Lions roar mainly at dawn and at sunset. Lions are usually standing when they roar, but they can also roar while sitting or lying down. They don't do it to scare prey. Lions roar to say "We are a family," "This area is ours," and "Other lions, stay away!" If male lions hear another lion roar near their pride, or even if they hear a zoologist's tape recording of a lion roaring, they immediately go to chase it away.

Another way lions claim their territory is by leaving their scent, or odor. Lions do this by urinating on the ground or rubbing against trees and bushes. They do this all throughout their territory, not just around its borders.

Besides hunting and protecting their territory, the main business of the pride is raising young. Usually, all the females in a pride are ready to mate at about the same time. That way all the cubs are born about the same time. They eat, sleep, play, and grow up together.

These females from a pride have become very good at hunting together.

The muscles of this female lion's back legs are very strong for leaping at prey.

When a lioness is ready to mate, she urinates more often. Her urine carries a special scent that tells the males she is ready. She also makes a long, low call that sounds like a rumble.

The first male to reach the female when she is ready is usually the one that gets to mate with her. If two males get there about the same time, they challenge each other. They turn their ears so the backs of them face forward. Their tails twitch and they lean forward and hiss at each other. Sometimes the weaker one gives up without fighting, but sometimes the stronger one must swat him with a heavy paw before he will leave. When one lion decides the other lion is stronger, his ears go flat against his head. He sinks to the ground and slowly crawls away.

The winning male guards his female and keeps her away from all the other males for several days. They don't eat during this time.

About 110 days after mating, the female gives birth. A week or so before this, she finds a sheltered place to use as a den site.

Lions usually don't have an actual den, like a cave or a tunnel into the ground. Instead they just need an area where the cubs are safe from storms and hidden from predators. It may be a place between boulders or under the overhanging edge of a dry riverbed.

A pride may use the same den site many times over the years, but they also stay alert for new sites that other animals don't know about yet.

Sometimes other animals discover the den site. Then the mother lion picks up each cub by the scruff of its neck and moves them all to a new den site.

If the new den site is not far, one or more of the cubs may walk on their own. Others may need help from their mother.

This den site is well protected from storms and well camouflaged from predators.

A mother lion may have as many as six cubs, but she usually has two or three. Each cub weighs just 2 to 4 pounds (0.9 to 1.8 kilograms). They are about the size of a soda-pop can, with stubby little legs. Their eyes stay closed until they are about 11 days old, and their first set of teeth comes in three to four weeks after birth.

Newborn cubs don't move much except to drink their mother's milk. The mother lion nurses her cubs for about eight hours every day. She keeps them warm by curling her body around them. She keeps them clean by licking up their urine and droppings. This keeps the den site from smelling and attracting hyenas or other predators that might kill the cubs.

During their first few weeks of life, the mother lion stays with her cubs most of the time. She only leaves when she needs to find food or water for herself. All the mother lions go hunting together. They are safer in a group. While the females hunt, they leave their cubs hidden in the den sites. The cubs stay very quiet.

## Lions
# FUNFACT:

**Both males and females roar, but males do it more often.**

The cubs can walk well by the time they are about five weeks old. Then their mother leads them away from their den site to join the rest of the pride. They meet the adults and other cubs, which become their playmates.

Every mother lion lets any cub in the group nurse from her. When she's awake, a mother may push away a cub that is not her own. But as soon as she dozes off, other cubs can snuggle up next to her and nurse from her.

Even with many adults around to protect them, more than half of the cubs die before they are one year old. Some are eaten by animals such as leopards. Some die of disease. If their mothers are having trouble finding food, they don't make enough milk, and the cubs starve.

As the survivors grow, their looks change, as well as what they eat, and what they are able to do for themselves.

When this mother takes her cub away from the den site,
she teaches it new things about the habitat.

Cubs don't learn everything from their mother. They also learn
many things from playing with each other.

At first, cubs have fuzzy brown or orange spots on their fluffy coats, which help to camouflage the cubs at the den site. Over time, the spots fade. Their coats become smooth and shiny. Young males grow long tufts of hair on their neck and shoulders. Eventually they develop a bushy mane like their fathers, but the mane won't be full size until the lions are about five years old.

At first, cubs get all their nourishment from their mother's milk. During this time, their mother brings dead prey near the cubs. She eats it in front of them so they can learn what adult lions eat. When they are about six weeks old, they start eating meat, too. Their baby teeth have come in so they are able to tear small pieces of meat. They continue to nurse until they are eight to ten months old, but they get more and more of their nourishment from meat.

When they are about six months old, their adult teeth start to come in. The cubs also start learning how to hunt. They follow along to watch how the females hunt.

Sometimes their mother brings them prey that she has injured, and lets them practice killing it. Often the cubs just want to play with the prey. At first, they don't know they must kill it in order to eat, but they soon understand what to do.

They learn to stalk silently by trying to sneak up on each other. They learn how to hide, how to wait patiently, and how to surprise their target by jumping out at just the right moment.

Hunting takes a lot of practice. Young lions don't kill prey on their own until they are at least 15 months old, and it takes many more weeks of practice before they are really good at it. Until then, they depend on their mother and the other adult females in the pride for their food.

One thing that makes hunting so hard to learn is that lions go after large animals that are big enough to fight back. They can bite, or strike out with their sharp hooves, or slash their pointed horns across a lion's tender belly. In order to be a good hunter, a lion must learn how to protect itself as well as how to find and kill the prey.

## Lions
# FUNFACT:

**Until about 10,000 years ago, lions could be found from Alaska and Yukon in North America to as far south as Peru in South America. They died out, or became extinct, because many of their prey animals became extinct.**

Before they are ready to go hunting with the rest of the pride,
cubs get practice by pretending to stalk and pounce on each other.

Finally, when they are two years old, the young lions can hunt for themselves. Young females stay with the pride. In two more years, they also will be ready to mate and raise a family.

Their brothers, however, are not allowed to stay with the pride. They are chased away by their mother. The young males from the pride usually stay together their whole life. They make up a group called a coalition (koe-uh-LIH-shun). Sometimes one male from another pride joins them. Their coalition lives and hunts together, and searches for a pride to join.

Like females in a pride, most males in a coalition are related.
A coalition may have only 2 members or as many as 9 members.

Male lions that are already with a pride don't want other males around, so when a new coalition comes along, they fight. The males bite and claw each other. Some of them even die.

If the pride lions win, life goes on as usual and the strangers go away. If the pride lions lose, they go off to live on their own. They will not live with a pride again. Soon, within a few months or a few years, they die.

The winning strangers kill all the cubs in the pride. Then, with those cubs out of the way, they mate with the females to produce cubs of their own. In some areas, more cubs die from being killed by male lions than from any other cause.

## Lions
# FUNFACT:

A male can eat 95 pounds
(43 kilograms) of meat in one day.
A female can eat 55 pounds
(25 kilograms).

Life is very dangerous for lions, especially for males and for cubs. Males that don't live with a pride constantly look for a pride to take over. Those that do live with a pride must always guard against coalitions trying to take their place. Male lions in eastern Africa live for about 12 years. In India, they live to be about 16 years old.

No matter which group of males wins the battles over the prides, lionesses stay in their birth pride. Females in eastern Africa and India live to be 18 years or older. They mate and raise cubs until they are 15 years old. They provide food for their pride and teach their offspring about hunting.

The male lion, with his magnificent mane and fearsome roar, may be "king." But the female, with her keen hunting and mothering skills, is the true center of the lion pride.

This healthy male and female are enjoying a good rest in their lush habitat.

# My BIG CATS! Adventures

The date of my adventure: _____

The people who came with me: _____

_____

Where I went: _____

What big cats I saw:

_____          _____

_____          _____

_____          _____

_____          _____

The date of my adventure: _____

The people who came with me: _____

_____

Where I went: _____

What big cats I saw:

_____          _____

_____          _____

_____          _____

_____          _____

# My BIG CATS! Adventures

The date of my adventure: _____

The people who came with me: _____

_____

Where I went: _____

What big cats I saw:

_____          _____

_____          _____

_____          _____

_____          _____

---

The date of my adventure: _____

The people who came with me: _____

_____

Where I went: _____

What big cats I saw:

_____          _____

_____          _____

_____          _____

_____          _____

*Explore the Fascinating World of . . .*

# Tigers

**Gwenyth Swain**
**Illustrations by John F. McGee**

WITH THEIR LARGE JAWS, powerful legs, and broad paws, tigers are really big! Male tigers can weigh over 670 pounds (300 kilograms). But with all their size, these great hunters move with the silence and grace of their relative the house cat. Tigers are one of 37 species (SPEE-sees), or kinds, of cats living on our planet today. Of all the different species of wild cats, tigers are the largest.

The tiger's scientific name is *Panthera tigris*. There are eight different groups, or subspecies (sub-SPEE-sees), of tigers. Over time, these different groups of tigers developed in different ways, depending on where they lived. Three subspecies of tiger are now extinct, or no longer living. They once prowled the islands of Java and Bali in Indonesia and the shores of the Caspian Sea in Asia.

Today, five subspecies of tigers roam areas of Asia from eastern Russia in the north to the island of Sumatra in the south. They are the Siberian (or Amur) tiger, the Sumatran tiger, the Indo-Chinese tiger, the South China tiger, and the Bengal (or Indian) tiger.

Tigers are the biggest cats in the world. Their powerful jaws and teeth are designed to crush bones and tear flesh.

Young tigers stay close to their mothers until they are about two years old.

Although the Siberian, or Amur, tiger's legs are shorter than those of other tiger subspecies, its paws are the largest.

Each subspecies looks a little different from the others. For example, the Siberian tiger lives in the Russian Far East. It has a heavy winter coat to help it survive in snowy surroundings. The Siberian tiger's thick, long fur sets it apart from tigers living in warmer places. While most tigers have black stripes, the Siberian tiger has brown stripes on a pale orange coat. Its underbelly is white to help it blend in with the snow on the ground. Its stripes blend in with bushes and trees.

Siberian tigers are the largest tigers of all. Males can weigh up to 675 pounds (304 kilograms) and are nearly 11 feet (3.3 meters) long. As with all other tiger subspecies, male Siberian tigers are bigger than females. But female Siberians are still big, weighing about 285 pounds (128 kilograms) on average. These tigers have to be large. They live in a colder climate than any other tiger subspecies, so they need a larger body, which can produce more heat. Over thousands of years, they have evolved, or changed, to have shorter legs and tails than other tiger subspecies, making it easier to keep warm.

Scientists who study animals are called zoologists (zoe-OL-uh-jists). They estimate that about 400 Siberian tigers live in the wild today.

## Tigers
# FUNFACT:

"White" tigers are just a rare color of tiger, not a different animal or subspecies. They are generally only found in zoos.

The tiger spends much of the day resting but is always alert to the sights and sounds of the animals it hunts for food.

The Sumatran tiger may be the smallest of the five subspecies, but it is still big. Even the smaller females weigh just under 200 pounds (90 kilograms)!

Sumatran tigers are the smallest tiger subspecies. Measuring about 8 feet (2.4 meters) from head to tail, male Sumatran tigers may weigh 265 pounds (120 kilograms), which is less than half the weight of their Siberian relatives!

Between 400 and 500 Sumatran tigers live in the wild, mainly in Sumatra's parks and reserves. The island of Sumatra is covered with hot and moist rain forests filled with lush, green plants. It makes a good habitat, or home, for these tigers.

The Sumatran tiger's fur helps it blend in with its surroundings. This is called camouflage (KAM-uh-flaj).

There is very little white in the dark orange coat, except for narrow bands of dirty white on the chest and belly. White would show up too clearly in the lush, green rain forest and make it more difficult for the tiger to travel without being seen. Stripes on the Sumatran tiger are black, and these tigers have more stripes, more closely packed together, than any other subspecies. Their stripes continue down the front legs, something not seen in Siberian tigers. Each tiger has a different pattern of stripes, and researchers sometimes use stripes to identify individual animals within a subspecies.

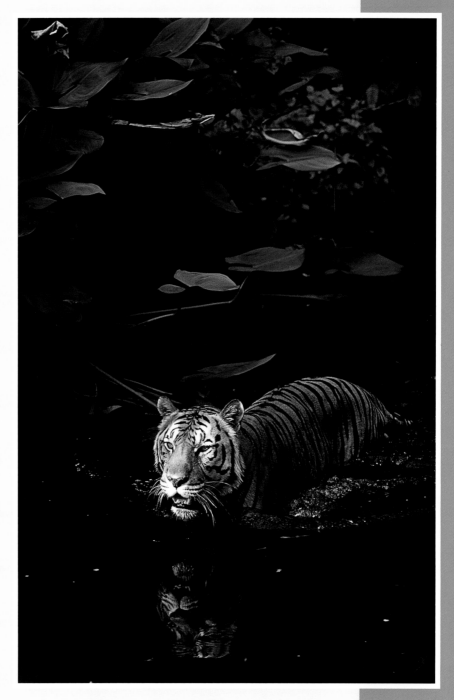

Unlike house cats, tigers spend quite a bit of time in the water—either cooling off, as this Sumatran tiger is doing, or hunting for food.

The Indo-Chinese tiger is found in more countries than any other tiger subspecies. About 1,500 of them are believed to live in the wild. They roam the hills and mountains of China, Myanmar (formerly Burma), Thailand, Cambodia, Laos, Vietnam, and Malaysia.

Indo-Chinese tigers are larger than their Sumatran relatives but still much smaller than Siberian tigers. Their coats are a warm, dark orange with black stripes. Indo-Chinese tigers have fewer stripes, farther apart, than Sumatran tigers but have more stripes and darker coats than their Siberian relatives.

No other tiger subspecies is in greater danger of becoming extinct, or dying out, than the South China tiger. Only 20 or 30 are thought to live in the wild. Male South China tigers are about 8 feet (2.4 meters) long and weigh about 330 pounds (150 kilograms). This tiger's orange coat has shorter, broader, and more openly spaced stripes than does the coat of the Siberian tiger.

Just as humans do, tigers learn by playing. Here, a young
Indo-Chinese tiger is play-fighting with its mother.

The tiger most people know is the Bengal tiger. These tigers live mainly in India, although some are found in Nepal, Bangladesh, Bhutan, and Myanmar. There are more tigers in India than in any other country in the world. Of the estimated 5,000 to 7,000 tigers in the wild, over half are Bengal tigers.

The average male Bengal tiger is about 9½ feet (2.9 meters) long and weighs about 480 pounds (220 kilograms). This tiger's dark orange coat with black stripes is similar to that of the Indo-Chinese tiger. The hair around its face is long, often making a "fringe."

The Bengal tiger's stripes are closer together than those of a South China tiger, and farther apart than those of a Sumatran tiger. Its underbelly fur is bright white, and it has fewer stripes on its front legs than a Sumatran tiger does. Without knowing where a tiger lives, however, even scientists have trouble telling different tiger subspecies apart.

Indo-Chinese tiger

South China tiger

Sumatran tiger

The face of this Bengal, or Indian, tiger is framed by a fringe of fur.

The Bengal tiger's habitat often has months of dry weather, so a pond like this one is essential to the animal's survival.

Tigers can live in many different kinds of habitats. While Siberian tigers thrive in snowy pine forests and Sumatran tigers prowl lush rain forests, Bengal tigers often live on dryer lands. Tigers in India live in grassy jungles and in forests with lakes. Indo-Chinese and South China tigers inhabit forests in remote hills or mountains.

Wherever tigers live, they need three important things. First, areas of thick trees and tall grasses are used as cover for hiding from enemies. Second, because tigers are carnivores (KAR-nuh-vorz), or meat eaters, they need lots of prey (PRAY). These are animals to hunt and eat. Third, tigers need a good supply of water to drink.

## Tigers
# FUNFACT:

According to Chinese tradition, the next "Year of the Tiger" will be in 2010.

A Sumatran tiger easily hides in the dense
growth of its rain forest habitat.

Adult tigers fight over territory, sometimes causing serious injury.

To find the things they need to survive, adult tigers may travel long distances, especially if prey animals are scarce. The area where a tiger lives and roams is called its territory. The size of a tiger's territory varies, depending on the number of prey animals that live there. A female Bengal tiger's territory may be about 10 square miles (26 square kilometers). Male tigers require larger territories, often overlapping those of several females.

Female Siberian tigers may have territories of well over 135 square miles (350 square kilometers)—more than 13 times the size of a female Bengal tiger's territory! Male Siberians range over even more land.

When a male tiger's territory overlaps those of females, the females may become mates for the male. Males often fight among themselves over the best territory and over mates. The losing male must leave the area to find another territory. The winning male stays in the area and mates with nearby females. Females usually spend all of their lives in the same territory. While female lions and their cubs live and hunt in groups known as prides, adult male tigers spend most of their lives alone.

Both males and females regularly travel through their territories, often at night. They may rest during the warm daylight hours in the same spot for several days in a row, but they rarely have a permanent home. A tiger's resting area is often a protected spot in tall grass or other good cover located near water. When a female tiger, or tigress, gives birth, she chooses an even more private spot, such as a cave, where she can hide her babies.

A young female tiger may live close to her mother's territory, but young males usually leave the area, sometimes settling far from their birthplace.

Adult tigers are so big that their only major predators (PRED-uh-torz), or enemies, are other tigers. Female tigers are smaller than males, but they are still very large animals. Female Bengal tigers, for example, weigh between 221 and 353 pounds (99–159 kilograms). That compares to between 419 and 569 pounds (189 and 256 kilograms) for the average male Bengal.

Much of that weight is muscle. A tiger's strong legs help it run in bursts of up to 35 miles (56 kilometers) per hour. They use their tails—3 to 4 feet (about 1 meter) of pure muscle—to help keep their balance while running and turning. Their powerful paws crash down on prey with great force.

## Tigers
# FUNFACT:

**Even though tigers prefer meat, they sometimes eat grass. It's probably to cure an upset stomach!**

A tiger's tail is about half as long as its body. While a tiger most often
uses its tail to maintain balance while running, it also uses
it to communicate with other tigers.

A Bengal tiger's sharp canine teeth are as long as the blade on a pocketknife and just as sharp.

A tiger's large jaws are strong enough to grab and hold prey. Some of their teeth, called canines (KAY-nines), are used to grab and bite prey animals. These teeth are very sharp and are located at the front of the upper and lower jaw. They may measure up to 3 inches (7.5 centimeters) long. If your upper canines were that long, they would reach below your chin! Tigers have a total of 30 teeth, compared to 32 in humans. Like other carnivores, tigers have razor-sharp back teeth called carnassials (kar-NASS-ee-uls). These teeth help tigers rip apart flesh and crush bones.

Tigers don't rely on just their size and strength for survival. Tigers have very good hearing, better than that of humans. Their ears can move to follow the sound of prey animals and predators. Their eyes seem to slant upward, with round black pupils and large yellow-orange irises. Tigers have the good eyesight you would expect from a relative of the house cat. In fact, a tiger's eyesight at night is about six times better than that of humans. Traveling at night is no problem for a tiger, especially when it combines its keen hearing and eyesight with its good sense of smell.

The tiger has an extremely good sense of smell, allowing it to sniff out its prey and to keep track of other tigers.

A tiger's snout ends with a sensitive orange-pink nose. Bristly whiskers extend from the tiger's cheek, adding to the animal's sense of touch. A tiger often uses its sense of smell to sniff out other tigers in or near its territory. Other tigers leave clues behind them. While traveling, they may stop to spray trees with their urine. They may rub their cheeks against trees or rocks, leaving scent (SENT), or odor, other tigers can smell. Or they may urinate or leave droppings, called scat, on the ground. These signs are ways tigers have of communicating their location, usually to let other male tigers know to stay away.

When a tigress is ready to mate, she marks her territory more often than usual. While marking, she makes a special sound to let any nearby males know that she is ready to mate.

Males may make several kinds of vocalizations (vo-kul-ize-A-shuns), or sounds. They growl, snarl, and even roar, usually to scare off other tigers or animals trying to steal food. Compared to lions, though, tigers don't roar very much. Generally tigers are quiet animals. Researchers believe that tigers, unlike house cats, do not purr when they are happy. This may be caused by differences in the two cats' throat bones.

## Tigers
# FUNFACT:

Pictures of tigers have appeared on postage stamps in countries around the world, including China, Canada, Sweden, and the United States.

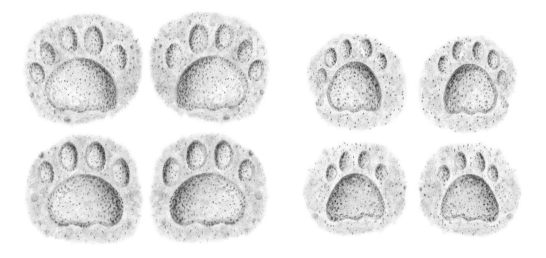

Male pugmarks                    Female pugmarks

Zoologists study tiger movements by looking at their paw prints, which are also called pugmarks. Pugmarks can be used to identify different subspecies. Prints from Siberian tigers, for example, are the biggest of any subspecies. Sumatran tigers have the smallest paw prints, averaging about 5 inches (13 centimeters) in length.

Pugmarks are also sometimes used to identify individual animals. Male tigers have bigger, wider, and more squared pugmarks than females. Some tigers have visible injuries to the five toes on their front feet or the four toes on their rear feet.

Claw marks are not visible in paw prints. Tigers use their sharp claws, which are about 3½ inches (9 centimeters) long, to climb short distances up trees to capture prey or to scratch trees when marking territory. But, like house cats, tigers retract, or pull in, their claws when not tearing or scratching. By studying tracks, researchers learn more about tiger travel and how tigers live.

Just as a house cat sharpens its claws on a carpet-covered "tree," this Bengal tiger claws tree bark. Claw marks set the boundaries for a tiger's territory.

Much of a tiger's time is spent sitting, lying down, and sleeping. Tigers are hard to see when they are at rest in tall grass, amid trees, or among thick bushes. Their stripes break up the outline of their orange coats, helping them blend in with their surroundings. When they stop to rest, tigers often groom themselves. They carefully lick clean their paws, chest, and back using their long, strong tongues. Tigers may then yawn a few times and rest or take a nap, but tigers don't stay in one place for long. As they crisscross their territory, they may take a quick drink in a pond or stream.

Because tigers are mainly active at night, when they do most of their hunting, they are called nocturnal (nok-TURN-ul) animals. If they feel safe, they may sometimes hunt during the daytime.

Whenever they choose to hunt, tigers must have patience. Only about 1 in 20 hunts is successful. Tigers increase their chances of success by watching their prey very carefully.

Tigers usually blend in with their surroundings, but this white tiger stands out wherever it goes. White tigers are a rare color form and not a separate subspecies. Because of their coloring, they generally do not survive long in the wild.

Young tigers, or cubs, often first learn to hunt by observing smaller prey. In India, for example, Bengal cubs begin by hunting langurs. These monkeys are safe from tigers when they stay high in the trees. But when the monkeys come out of the trees to drink at watering holes, cubs are already waiting, hidden in the grasses. When the time is right, the cub pounces, or suddenly jumps out of its hiding place. If it is lucky, the cub will surprise the monkey and make it a meal.

The Bengal tiger's favorite prey animal is the sambar, a type of large deer. Siberian tigers eat the Siberian wapiti, a kind of elk. But tigers don't hunt just one kind of prey. Bengal tigers, for example, also hunt wild boar, wild cattle, monkeys, and peacocks.

Tigers may eat almost any kind of meat if they are hungry enough. From the presence of quills in tiger scat, we know that tigers eat porcupines. Encounters with porcupines—and their long, sharp quills—can cause serious injury to tigers. Tigers also may eat other tigers.

Six-month-old Bengal tiger cubs are about the size of a large dog—
big enough to begin learning to hunt on their own.

Tigers use several different methods when hunting and killing their prey. Often tigers select a daytime resting place close to a source of water. As the day grows warmer, other animals come to the lake or stream. If they are thirsty enough, they take the risk of exposing themselves to a tiger's attack in order to get a drink of cooling water. Some animals wait to drink at night. But tigers are watching and waiting then, too.

When hunting, a tiger may simply remain in one place and wait until its prey has wandered close by. Or it may slowly and silently stalk, or sneak up on, its prey. The soft, cushioning pads on the bottoms of its paws help the tiger move very quietly. Once close enough, the tiger pounces and attacks. When tigers chase their prey, they can leap at least 15 feet (4.5 meters) in one bound.

## Tigers
# FUNFACT:

Tigers are good swimmers. They cool off in water during hot weather. They also stalk prey in ponds and streams, sometimes swimming many yards, but tigers don't like to get their heads wet. They usually go into the water tail first.

After a long night of hunting, a Bengal tiger still stalks prey along the water's edge.

Tigers may leap, lunge, and pounce many times before they capture prey.
Only five percent of hunts are successful.

Bengal tigers are very successful in hunting their main prey animal, the sambar, by stalking and pouncing. Sambars have an excellent sense of smell, but their eyesight is poor compared to that of the tiger. As long as a tiger can stay out of the wind and keep its scent from getting to the sambar's nose, it has a good chance of capturing its prey. When a sambar does smell a tiger, it bellows. That alarm call tells the whole herd to flee, or run away.

If the tiger catches the sambar before it starts to bellow, it usually kills the animal with its powerful jaws. While a blow from a tiger's paw can stun a smaller prey animal, the sambar is large and fast. It must be stopped in another way. Tigers usually leap upon the sambar and sink their long canine teeth into the animal's neck. Then they quickly swing the body from side to side until the animal stops moving. Sambar and other large prey usually die when the tiger's grip on the neck makes breathing impossible. Tigers sometimes manage to break the necks of smaller prey first.

After the kill, a tiger drags the prey's body, or carcass, into the shelter of tall grass or woods. It wants to be sure that no other animal will find and steal its kill. Tigers may leave the area briefly to find water, but they are very protective of their kills. When possible, a tiger covers the carcass with sticks or branches to hide it from scavenger animals, such as vultures, and other tigers.

When it comes to eating, the tiger is efficient and leaves little to waste. It uses its canine teeth to tear the meat from the bones. A tiger usually feeds on a larger animal starting from the hind end. When the meat is gone, the tiger may use its strong jaws to crush and eat the smaller bones. During times of drought, or a long period of very dry weather, the wet marrow inside the bones provides tigers with an important source of liquid.

This kind of eating is hard work. Tigers generally eat for an hour or so before resting. A tiger continues to eat and sleep near its prey until all the meat is gone, even if it takes several days. In one night, a tiger can eat as much as 50 pounds (23 kilograms) of meat!

If a larger tiger challenges a smaller one over a carcass, the smaller tiger will usually leave, but not without a fight. One or both of them may be seriously injured. Tigers prefer not to feed together, except when a female shares a kill with her cubs.

## Tigers
# FUNFACT:

Tigers can kill prey animals weighing up to 2,200 pounds (about 1,000 kilograms), many times their own weight.

Tigers do not usually share carcasses with other adults,
but mother tigers share with their cubs.

A mother watches over her young. Cubs face many dangers—illness, starvation, and attack. Scientists believe that of every 100 cubs born, only 50 will survive.

A tigress is ready to mate when she is 3½ to 4 years old. Tigers can mate at any time of the year but are more likely to mate in the cool season. For Bengal tigers, mating usually takes place from November to April. After mating, the male takes no more interest in the female or in raising the family.

Before she gives birth, the female often chooses a cave or other hidden place for her den. The cubs will be almost helpless at birth. She must be sure they will be safe from predators and protected from the weather.

Female tigers are very successful at keeping their babies out of sight. In fact, zoologists have rarely seen cubs younger than three or four months old in the wild. Most of what we know about the early weeks of a tiger's life comes from studies of animals in zoos.

The cubs are born about three months after mating. Tigers generally give birth to litters, or groups, of two to four cubs. Whatever the size of the litter, the number of male and female cubs is usually equal. Soon after birth, the mother licks her babies' fur clean. This licking helps a cub's digestion and blood circulation start working properly. Grooming also keeps the cubs clean so their new scent will not attract predators.

Cubs born in the wild are rarely seen during the first few months of life. A tigress keeps her litter well hidden until the cubs begin to defend themselves.

Newborn tigers weigh about 2 or 3 pounds (about 1 kilogram). Their eyes remain closed for 3 to 14 days after they are born. Even then, they don't see well until they are several weeks old. Cubs nurse, or drink milk, from their mother. Cubs add meat to their diets when they are around six to eight weeks old, but they may continue to nurse until they are about one year old.

Keeping up her strength while nursing and providing meat to cubs is hard work for a mother tiger. She may have to leave her cubs to hunt as often as every other day. Until they are a few months old, the cubs stay close to the protection of the den. If a mother tiger thinks that her den is no longer safe, she moves her cubs to a new site, or location. When her babies are very small, she gently picks them up, one by one, with her teeth and carries them to their new den.

To keep her young cubs safe, a mother may only allow them to leave the den with her at night. Smaller cats, such as leopards, will attack unprotected cubs. Male tigers are another threat. If a male tiger thinks that cubs are not his offspring, he may try to kill them. This is just one more way for a male tiger to protect his territory. A mother tiger warns her cubs of danger by making high, squeaky noises or soft grunts.

Cubs can crawl through thick bushes and grasses before they are about two weeks old. Beginning when they are three or four months old, cubs may be led out of the den to share the mother's kill. They also will play among themselves, pretending to stalk each other like prey and then pouncing.

By the time the cubs are about six months old, they are the size of large dogs. They have learned many things, such as how to find their own mother by following her scent in case they become lost.

Tigers use their tongues for grooming, or keeping clean.

181

Young cubs often follow their mother and quietly watch her hunt. As they grow older, the cubs begin to stalk and hunt, too. A mother may injure her prey and allow her cubs to finish off the kill. That way, the cubs learn important hunting skills.

By the time they are 1½ years old, the cubs have gotten their permanent teeth. Now they are able to make their own kills. They spend more and more time away from their mother. They explore streams and ponds where prey go for water. They follow trails and paths around their mother's territory, learning the landscape. They play and hunt among themselves.

When they are about two years old, the cubs leave their mother's territory to find a territory of their own. Sometimes two or more cubs from the same litter may travel and live together for a short time after they leave their mother. But soon they begin to live the solitary life of the tiger. Tigers in the wild usually live to be about 10 to 15 years old.

A Siberian tiger plays with her cub in a stream.

All five tiger subspecies are endangered. Only conservation programs can ensure the survival of these fierce and beautiful creatures.

Tigers today live in parts of the world where the human population is growing rapidly. All tiger subspecies are endangered, which means they are in danger of dying out.

Thousands of Siberian, Indo-Chinese, and other tigers have been hunted and killed illegally so their bones could be used in traditional Chinese medicine. For many years in India, Bengal tigers have competed for land with cattle herders. In the mid-1900s, the tiger populations were decreasing rapidly. A program called Project Tiger began to reverse that trend in the 1980s. The program established several parks and reserves where tigers are protected. Bengal tiger populations increased in the late 1980s and 1990s. Siberian tiger habitats in Russia also are being protected with the hope that tiger numbers there will soon increase.

Fortunately, many people are working hard to study and protect the endangered tiger. The more we know about these beautiful and powerful animals, the more likely they will survive for centuries to come.

# My BIG CATS! Adventures

The date of my adventure: _____

The people who came with me: _____

_____

Where I went: _____

What big cats I saw:

_____        _____

_____        _____

_____        _____

_____        _____

The date of my adventure: _____

The people who came with me: _____

_____

Where I went: _____

What big cats I saw:

_____        _____

_____        _____

_____        _____

_____        _____

# My BIG CATS! Adventures

The date of my adventure: _____

The people who came with me: _____

_____

Where I went: _____

What big cats I saw:

_____          _____

_____          _____

_____          _____

_____          _____

The date of my adventure: _____

The people who came with me: _____

_____

Where I went: _____

What big cats I saw:

_____          _____

_____          _____

_____          _____

# COUGARS Index

# LEOPARDS Index

# LIONS Index

# TIGERS Index